SONNETS
TO ORPHEUS

To my friend

Adrial,

love

Robert

RAINER MARIA RILKE
SONNETS
TO ORPHEUS

TRANSLATED AND WITH AN INTRODUCTION BY
DAVID YOUNG

WESLEYAN UNIVERSITY PRESS

LIBRARY OF CONGRESS
CATALOGING-IN-PUBLICATION DATA
Rilke, Rainer Maria, 1875–1926.
  Sonnets to Orpheus.
  (Wesleyan poetry in translation)
  Translation of: Die Sonette an Orpheus.
  Bibliography: p.
  I. Young, David, 1936–   . II. Title
III. Series.
PT2635.I65S613   1987   831'.912   87-6146
ISBN 0-8195-5159-7 (alk. paper)
ISBN 0-8195-6165-7 (pbk. : alk. paper)

All inquiries and permissions requests should be addressed to the
Publisher, University Press of New England, Hanover, New Hampshire
03755.

Manufactured in the United States of America

WESLEYAN POETRY IN TRANSLATION

5   4

Cover photo: Rilke in Hotêl Biron, courtesy Fischer-Verlag

CONTENTS

INTRODUCTION

In February 1922, Rainer Maria Rilke recovered his creative energies as a poet with a suddenness and abundance virtually unparalleled in the history of poetic composition. The resulting masterpieces—the *Duino Elegies*, a long-standing project, and the unplanned *Sonnets to Orpheus*—were in one respect a bolt from the blue and in another the result of patient effort and unswerving purpose. The poet's imagination had finally mended a world that was shattered by World War One, completing a bridge to his own artistic career and creative self, stranded on the far side of Europe's cataclysmic upheavals nearly ten years before. Rilke had to leave Germany (he had spent most of the war in Munich, some of it in military service), settle in Switzerland, find a congenial place to live and work (the medieval tower at Muzot), and reawaken his emotions with a passionate love affair. After these things had been accomplished, along with a visit to his beloved Paris and a re-exposure to the French literature (particularly the poetry of Valéry) he cared so deeply for, Rilke was ready to write. When the poems came, they were a veritable avalanche. Especially gratifying, because unforeseen, were the poems of the great two-part sonnet sequence presented here.

Rilke had long since mastered the sonnet as a literary form, but the *Orpheus* is his first (and only) sonnet *sequence,* a form whose characteristics and tradition it will be profitable to glance at as a preliminary to consideration of this poem. A sonnet sequence may be seen as a series of individual poems linked by common themes, by their study of a specific situation or relationship, or even simply by the occasion of their writing, i.e., covering a specific period of a writer's life. But a sonnet sequence may also be thought of as a long poem; when that perspective is used, the individual sonnets act as stanzas, and, when narrative is present, as episodes. The fact that a sonnet sequence occupies a sort of middle ground between the long poem and the loose collection of individual lyrics makes it something of a risk, but it also creates, for both reader and writer, a potential advantage, since it combines diversity with unity.

Most of the great sonnet sequences are built around a love relationship. The love may be unsuccessful in terms of wordly judgment, but the otherwordly is never very far away. From Petrarch on, the painful ways of human emotion, its frustrations and bewilderments, have been a window to the infinite, a means of discovering the universal power of love. Moreover, in the process of documenting the ups and downs of a relationship, the poet-lover may range quite widely for topics, moods, occasions and ideas. The amount of attention that Shakespeare devotes to the problems of time and change in his sonnet sequence is a familiar instance of a widespread tendency.

Rilke appears to have seized on this expansiveness in achieving and designing his sequence, as well as on the lover's pilgrimage to mystical knowledge. He does not center his poem on love for a particular person, but writes instead a kind of extended love-poem to the world, celebrating such diverse love-objects as mirrors, dogs, fruit, ancient sarcophagi, roses, a strip of cloth, unicorns, breathing and childhood. Thus the expansiveness and diversity of the traditional sequence are extended, and the narrative base provided by the history of a specific relationship virtually disappears. I say virtually because this sequence of sonnets does have two recurrent figures who are addressed frequently enough to raise the possibility that the entire poem is devoted to either or both of them: the god Orpheus, prototype of the poet, and the young dancer, Vera Ouckama Knoop, whose death is treated elegiacally. These characters seem in one sense to replace Petrarch's Laura or Sidney's Stella, but in another sense they take their place among the crowd of subjects the poet confronts when he asks himself what a given sonnet might celebrate or meditate upon. The sonnets can be "to" Orpheus because the possibility of poetry is everywhere in the world, and they can be "to" or "for" the young dancer because her death, in effect, merges her with that world. But they are a kind of manual on how to approach the world, how to see and understand its myriad forms and activities. If, as I've suggested elsewhere, the *Duino Elegies* are about what it really means to be human, the sonnets seem to be about how you can love the world, and survive in it, given that condition.

I first heard about these poems, I realize, as an undergraduate in the nineteen-fifties, when my German teacher told us that there was a modern German poet who actually talked about having a tree inside his ear. How was one supposed to understand that? The teacher's literal-mindedness shows how slowly poetry sometimes makes its way in this world, but it also illustrates the way in which Rilke confronts his reader immediately with a breakdown of the normal distinctions between inside and outside, self and world. One can rather uneasily write off the tall tree in the ear as a figure of speech for Orpheus's majestic music, but the second sonnet, in which a sleeping girl "made a bed for herself inside my ear," leaves us no choice but to abandon our normal distinctions between the subjective and the objective. Somehow the god and the girl are both within and without the poet-speaker. In taking all of existence inside himself, or distributing himself across all of existence, he jeopardizes his identity and coherence, but he promises us a magical pilgrimage, a time of heightened awareness and personal liberation. It is a promise the sequence makes good on.

In a sonnet sequence, the relation of poem to poem presents various possibilities, from close linkage to abrupt transition, with the further option of poems that echo each other from a distance. Rilke's sequence explores these options in quite interesting ways. There are "groups" that take up a common subject and lead into each other: a "fruit" group, 12–15 of Part One, and a "flower" group, 5–7 in Part Two. There are sonnets dealing with the season of spring that linked together (24 and 25 of Part Two) and that in turn echo sonnets with the same topic from earlier in the sequence (21 of Part One and, in a sense, 20 as well). Since the sequence has two main parts, a natural consequence is the pairing of sonnets from the first part with sonnets from the second. Rilke avoids excessive symmetry, but one of his most interesting pairs are the sonnet about the Roman sarcophagi (I, 10) and the one about the ancient fountain (II, 15). The three sonnets that deal satirically and rather nervously with the human infatuation with machinery in Part One (18, 23 and 24) are matched with a more confident treatment of the subject in II, 10. And so it goes. Again and again in Part Two the reader will find deliberate and felicitous echoes of Part One.

Sometimes the transition from one sonnet to the next will strike the reader initially as jarring, only to make its imaginative logic clear on further inspection. In Part Two, for example, the transition from 6 to 7 is very clear, since the former is about the rose and the latter about cut flowers. The next poem, about childhood, seems less connected until we reflect on the parallel between child and flower. Then, in 9, there seems to be an abrupt change of subject and tone, a poem that mocks and attacks legalistic views of existence and past and present forms of punishment and justice. But the poem closes by using the image of a child "quietly playing," as a simile for merciful feelings, and thus connects firmly with the previous sonnet after all. This group of four helps to illustrate the quite various ways in which Rilke is capable of connecting his sonnets. It is easy to underestimate their fundamental unity.

Indeed, the entire poem can be said to find a surprising unity in the essential duality of existence. The spiritual and the material worlds, the divine and the human, togetherness and separateness: these facts of existence are again and again pointed out in these poems, and the two-part structure seems to confirm a fundamental duality in existence. Like the poem, we have bilateral symmetry and a tendency to think in binary oppositions and pairings. The subject of the sequence is dual—the god and the young dead dancer—as is the basic form of the sonnet, with its octave and sestet. The sonnet traditionally goes in one direction and then "turns." (The Italians called the transition from the octave to sestet the "volta," a change of direction.) Like the human mind itself, "hesitating between," everything divides, threatening to remain separate, and the poem's great strength lies partly in its ready admission of that: "The human self is split; where two / heartways cross, there is no temple to Apollo." Out of the nettle of duality, however, Rilke plucks the flower of unity, finding ways, again and again, of closing the fissured self, healing the god/man and spirit/matter splits, so that the entire sequence becomes a giant demonstration of the rhythms of dividing and uniting, wounding and healing, rhythms that the poet feels must characterize experience. The insight also becomes a justification for change. The instability of experience leads to fissuring and self-division, but transformation (featured on the mythic level as metamorphosis) can also go the other way, uniting what has been divided. The double form of the sequence, then, along with its manner at every level, is thus an essential part of the truth and force of the poet's vision.

Beyond its brilliant structure and innovative use of tradition, the *Sonnets to Orpheus* has rhetorical and stylistic felicities that deserve attention here. They stamp the sequence not only as Rilke's work, but as late Rilke, that is, as a poetry of extraordinary imaginative power.

One striking feature of Rilke's imagination is its power of entering sympathetically into its subjects. Such an ability is appropriate to a sonnet sequence that explores love not just for another human being or a god but for a wide assortment of objects and situations, some of them rather unlikely. It is the way the poet makes his claims good, validates the strength of his feeling. His imagination circles his subjects lovingly, and melts into them, again breaking down the subject-object distinction. It is a technique he had developed in the *Neue Gedichte* (*New Poems,* 1908), many of which are also sonnets. When it succeeds, we see existence in new ways, from viewpoints and states of being that were closed off to us previously. Thus, for example, Rilke imagines what it might be like to be a cut flower:

> you
> who lay on the garden table, often from rim to
> rim, weary and mildly wounded

awaiting the water that would revive you
from death, already begun—, and now
lifted again between the streaming poles
of feeling fingers . . .

(II,7)

This is not sentimental pathos or even anthropomorphizing. The power of sympathy here, the successful attempt to imagine what fingers would seem like to a cut flower, is akin to what Keats praised in Shakespeare as "negative capability"; the poet suppresses his own selfhood in order to facilitate his imaginative transformation into the object of his attention. Rilke's innovation with this poetic norm lies in the scope and variety of things he is able to treat in this way: mirrors, breathing, fish, and concepts (grief, praise) as well.

Again and again, Rilke startles us with his ability to bring physical and spiritual together, to make them interchange qualities and meanings. Sometimes he accomplishes these "marriages" by especially apt comparisons:

Here in the kingdom of decay, among what's wasting,
be a tinkling glass that shatters itself with sound.

(II,13)

This is part of a general set of advice ("Be ahead of all partings") on how to deal with change, so that we understand its abstract meaning. What makes it effective, however, is the precision with which we are allowed to understand it through the imaginative detail of the tinkling glass and its self-shattering. A glass that could shatter itself before destructive sound-waves reached it has never existed, but we can make it exist in the imagination and extrapolate its meaning because of the careful placement of the image and the powerful articulation of the poet's imagination. We forget the usual demarcations of material ("kingdom") and conceptual ("decay") when under the spell of such magic, and the visible and invisible worlds coexist effortlessly for us. Rilke uses every sort of poetic figurative device—metonymy, personification, simile, oxymoron, etc.—to make the coexistence possible.

The reader is often startled too by the speed with which the poet's imagination moves forward. Sonnet 10 of Part One is about some ancient Roman sarcophagi that have been used as watering troughs for a long time:

> You've never been away from me, antique
> sarcophagi, but I greet you—you
> whom jubilant waters have flowed through
> since Roman days, as wandering music.

We have already, as the objects are introduced, to deal with some departures from the norm: greeting something that has not been absent (as part of greeting an inanimate object at all!) and water as music. Even as we make these adjustments, the subject changes:

> Or those old graves, wide open, like the eyes
> of a shepherd who wakes feeling joyful,
> —full of stillness and blossoming nettles—
> releasing a swarm of elated butterflies . . .

Now we have a twin subject, and a natural pairing—the sarcophagi and some similar open graves or tombs (we know from a letter that Rilke had in mind some empty tombs near Arles). The transition is not difficult but the simile that we are given—open graves compared to the eyes of someone who has just waked up—is both surprising and exhilarating, and the three "realistic" details (stillness and nettles, a typical abstract/concrete pairing, and the swarm of butterflies) match that mood precisely, so that the simile is less distinct from the main subject than it would normally be.

Having established the subject (addressing empty graves as remarkable friends) and made the eye comparison, Rilke can go on, in the first part of the sestet, to a "mouth comparison":

> all that we snatch away from doubt
> I greet, mouths that are open once more,
> having learned what silence means.

Mouths are for eating, speaking, singing. They can be for silence and absence, too. Having addressed and understood these ineffable mouths, devourers of the dead and singers (through silence) of ultimate reconciliation, Rilke swings back to human experience, which is more familiar, but more ambiguous and divided:

> Have *we* learned that? Or have we yet
> to learn? Both. Hesitating between
> is what gives our faces character.

The earlier eyes and mouths help make the final images of the face, molded by experience, seem natural, even inevitable. Again, the essential unity of Rilke's enterprise strikes us gradually, when we have had time to consider the remarkable curves and planes of his unpredictable but solid structures.

The marriages of man and god, concrete and abstract, grief and celebration, changelessness and change, and other such contraries, make the reading of *The Sonnets to Orpheus* a challenging and difficult matter. They also, of course, pose problems for the translator. When I undertook this translation, some years back and after treating the *Duino Elegies* to a rather unorthodox handling, I had the notion that I need not be bound to reflect Rilke's choice of the sonnet form. I might, for example, translate these great and difficult lyrics into prose poems! I discovered, as I worked, that the meaning and the expressiveness of these poems are completely bound up with the possibilities of their form, the sonnet and its larger manifestation, the sonnet sequence; no translator can afford to ignore that fact. The next problem, then, was how to make sonnets in English that would honor Rilke's choice of form but still feel contemporary, or at least modern. Some translators—M. D. Herter Norton, Robert Bly—have chosen to produce unrhymed sonnets, while others—Leishman, MacIntyre—have tried to replicate the rhymes. I chose the middle ground of off-rhyme (also called "near rhyme" and "touch-rhyme"), which allowed me many more choices of diction and syntax than full rhyme would have, and which helped me hold the poems to their original commitments to a traditional form without making that commitment obtrusive in English. Many readers will not even notice the "rhyme schemes" of these poems; that aspect is intended to remain in the background.

Despite their faintness and "dissonance," my rhymes helped me hold the translations to their forms and the implication of those forms, without too much distortion. In the sonnet just discussed, for example, I have rhymed "antique" and "music," "you" and "through" (sometimes the rhymes are full), "eyes" and "butterflies," "joyful" and "nettles," "doubt" and "yet," "more" and "character," and "means" and "between." That is fairly typical. The point, for me, is that I have not had to make my choices in order to achieve those rhymes—the tail has not wagged the dog. Where I handled the poem rather freely, in the final tercet (the reader can find a more literal version in the Herter Norton translation), it was not from the necessity of replicating the formal rhyme scheme, but in order to try to match in English something of the speed and naturalness of the original. There is a fruitful tension in Rilke's sonnets between predictability and spontaneity, and a translator needs to try to be faithful to it. Neither unrhymed nor fully rhymed versions of the sonnets seemed to me to capture that tension.

These translations were first published serially in *FIELD*, in the Fall 1978 and Spring 1979 issues. They have been out of print for some time now, and I have received enough requests for copies and suggestions that I republish them to feel it is time to commit them to book form, along with this introduction and some notes. No doubt they have shortcomings—Rilke is very difficult to capture—but they strive to reflect the spirit and manner of the original, itself a somewhat uneven and bewildering experience for the reader. *The Sonnets to Orpheus* is, however, one of the great modern poems, not to mention a monumental addition to the literature of the sonnet sequence, and the enterprise of bringing it over into our language in an expressive and contemporary version is surely worth the risk.

My work on Rilke has benefited greatly from the advice and support of a number of people, including Richard Exner, Marjorie Hoover, David Walker, and Chloe Young. Most notable, however, has been the friendship, enthusiasm and expertise of Stuart Friebert. To him, with thanks, I dedicate this translation.

FIRST PART

1

Da stieg ein Baum. O reine Übersteigung!
O Orpheus singt! O hoher Baum im Ohr!
Und alles schwieg. Doch selbst in der Verschweigung
ging neuer Anfang, Wink und Wandlung vor.

Tiere aus Stille drangen aus dem klaren
gelösten Wald von Lager und Genist;
und da ergab sich, dass sie nicht aus List
und nicht aus Angst in sich so leise waren,

sondern aus Hören. Brüllen, Schrei, Geröhr
schien klein in ihren Herzen. Und wo eben
kaum eine Hütte war, dies zu empfangen,

ein Unterschlupf aus dunkelstem Verlangen
mit einem Zugang, dessen Pfosten beben,—
da schufst du ihnen Tempel im Gehör.

1

A tree stood up. Oh pure uprising!
Orpheus is singing! Oh tall tree in the ear!
And everything grew still. Yet in the silence there
changes took place, signals and fresh beginnings.

Creatures of stillness crowded from the clear
untangled woods, from nests and lairs;
and it turned out that their light
stepping came not from fear or from cunning

but so they could listen. Shriek, bellow and roar
had shrunk in their hearts. And while before
there was scarcely a hut where they might stay,

just a shelter made of the darkest cravings
with shaky posts for an entranceway—
you made a temple for them in their hearing.

2

Und fast ein Mädchen wars und ging hervor
aus diesem einigen Glück von Sang und Leier
und glänzte klar durch ihre Frühlingsschleier
und machte sich ein Bett in meinem Ohr.

Und schlief in mir. Und alles war ihr Schlaf.
Die Bäume, die ich je bewundert, diese
fühlbare Ferne, die gefühlte Wiese
und jedes Staunen, das mich selbst betraf.

Sie schlief die Welt. Singender Gott, wie hast
du sie vollendet, dass sie night begehrte,
erst wach zu sein? Sieh, sie erstand und schlief.

Wo ist ihr Tod? O, wirst du dies Motiv
erfinden noch, eh sich dein Lied verzehrte?—
Wo sinkt sie hin aus mir? . . . Ein Mädchen fast . . .

2

From the joined happiness of song and lyre
a girl, almost, was formed, came forth, glowed
clearly through her April veils, and made
a bed for herself inside my ear.

And slept in me. And then her sleep was
everything: trees I had wondered at, those
vivid distances, the meadow I felt, every
amazement that had ever been inside me.

She slept the world. Singing god, how did
you make her so whole she didn't first
need to be awake? See, she rose up, still asleep.

Where's her death? Do you have time to find
that subject before your song burns up?
Where does she drain out of me? . . . a girl, almost . . .

3

Ein Gott vermags. Wie aber, sag mir, soll
ein Mann ihm folgen durch die schmale Leier?
Sein Sinn ist Zwiespalt. An der Kreuzung zweier
Herzwege steht kein Tempel für Apoll.

Gesang, wie du ihn lehrst, ist nicht Begehr,
nicht Werbung um ein endlich noch Erreichtes;
Gesang ist Dasein. Für den Gott ein Leichtes.
Wann aber *sind* wir? Und wann wendet er

an unser Sein die Erde und die Sterne?
Dies *ists* nicht, Jüngling, dass du liebst, wenn auch
die Stimme dann den Mund dir aufstösst,—lerne

vergessen dass du aufsangst. Das verrinnt.
In Wahrheit singen, ist ein andrer Hauch.
Ein Hauch um nichts. Ein Wehn im Gott. Ein Wind.

3

A god can do it. But tell me how
a man can follow him through the narrow
lyre. The human self is split; where two
heartways cross, there is no temple to Apollo.

Song, as you teach it, is not desire, not
a wooing of something that's finally attained;
song is existence. Easy for the god. But
when do *we* exist? And when does he spend

the earth and the stars on our being?
When we love? That's what you think when you're young;
not so, though your voice forces open your mouth,—

learn to forget how you sang. That fades.
Real singing is a different kind of breath.
A nothing-breath. A ripple in the god. A wind.

4

O ihr Zärtlichen, tretet zuweilen
in den Atem, der euch nicht meint,
lasst ihn an eueren Wangen sich teilen,
hinter euch zittert er, wieder vereint.

O ihr Seligen, o ihr Heilen,
die ihr der Anfang der Herzen scheint.
Bogen der Pfeile und Ziele von Pfeilen,
ewiger glänzt euer Lächeln verweint.

Fürchtet euch nicht zu leiden, die Schwere,
gebt sie zurück an der Erde Gewicht;
schwer sind die Berge, schwer sind die Meere.

Selbst die als Kinder ihr pflanztet, die Bäume,
wurden zu schwer längst; ihr trüget sie nicht.
Aber die Lüfte . . . aber die Räume . . .

4

You should step, sometimes, you gentle ones,
into the breath that pays you no mind;
let it part against your cheeks and then,
quivering, rejoin itself behind.

Oh blessed ones, oh perfect ones,
who seem like the origins of hearts;
bows for the arrows as well as their targets,
how long and far a tear-stained smile shines.

Don't be afraid to suffer. Heaviness
you can give back to the weight of the planet;
mountains are heavy, seas are heavy too.

Even the trees you carried to plant
as children, have long since been too heavy for you.
Oh, but the open air . . . oh, but the empty spaces . . .

5

Errichtet keinen Denkstein. Lasst die Rose
nur jedes Jahr zu seinen Gunsten blühn.
Denn Orpheus ists. Seine Metamorphose
in dem und dem. Wir sollen uns nicht mühn

um andre Namen. Ein für alle Male
ists Orpheus, wenn es singt. Er kommt und geht.
Ists nicht schon viel, wenn er die Rosenschale
um ein paar Tage manchmal übersteht?

O wie er schwinden muss, dass ihrs begrifft!
Und wenn ihm selbst auch bangte, dass er schwände.
Indem sein Wort das Hiersein übertrifft,

ist er schon dort, wohin ihrs nicht begleitet.
Der Leier Gitter zwängt ihm nicht die Hände.
Und er gehorcht, indem er überschreitet.

5

Don't lay a stone to his memory. The rose
can bloom, if you like, once a year for his sake.
For Orpheus *is* the rose. His metamorphosis
takes this form, that form. No need to think

about his other names. Once and for all:
when there's singing, it's Orpheus. He comes and goes.
It's enough if sometimes he stays several
days; more, say, than a bowl of roses.

He has to vanish so you can understand.
Even if it frightens him to disappear.
While his word is transforming our beings here

he's somewhere else, past following.
The lyre's grill doesn't pinch his hands.
Even as he breaks rules, he's obeying.

6

Ist er ein Hiesiger? Nein, aus beiden
Reichen erwuchs seine weite Natur.
Kundiger böge die Zweige der Weiden,
wer die Wurzeln der Weiden erfuhr.

Geht ihr zu Bette, so lasst auf dem Tische
Brot nicht und Milch nicht; die Toten ziehts—.
Aber er, der Beschwörende, mische
unter der Milde des Augenlids

ihre Erscheinung in alles Geschaute;
und der Zauber von Erdrauch und Raute
sei ihm so wahr wie der klarste Bezug.

Nichts kann das gültige Bild ihm verschlimmern;
sei es aus Gräbern, sei es aus Zimmern,
rühme er Fingerring, Spange und Krug.

6

Is he of this world? No, he gets
his large nature from both realms. To know
how best to curve the willow's boughs
you have to have been through its roots.

Don't leave bread or milk on the table
at night: that attracts the dead.
But under your own mild eyelids
you can let this conjuror mingle

the sight of the dead into all that you've seen;
and may the magic of earthsmoke and meadow rue
be as true as the clearest relation.

Nothing should spoil good images; whether
they came from a grave or a bedroom,
let him praise finger-ring, buckle, and pitcher.

7

Rühmen, das ists! Ein zum Rühmen Bestellter,
ging er hervor wie das Erz aus des Steins
Schweigen. Sein Herz, o vergängliche Kelter
eines den Menschen unendlichen Weins.

Nie versagt ihm die Stimme am Staube,
wenn ihn das göttliche Beispiel ergreift.
Alles wird Weinberg, alles wird Traube,
in seinem fühlenden Süden gereift.

Nicht in den Grüften der Könige Moder
straft ihm die Rühmung Lügen, oder
dass von den Göttern ein Schatten fällt.

Er ist einer der bleibenden Boten,
der noch weit in die Türen der Toten
Schalen mit rühmlichen Früchten hält.

7

Praising, that's it! Praise was his mission,
and he came the way ore comes, from silent
rock. His heart, a wine press that couldn't last
made us an endless supply of wine.

Even in the dust his voice won't fail him
once the godhead has him in its grip.
All things turn vineyard, all things turn grape,
in the ripening South of his feelings.

Nothing can contradict his praise,
not mold in the royal burial vault
nor the fact that a shadow will fall from the gods.

He's the messenger who stays,
who carries his bowls of praiseworthy fruit
across the thresholds of the dead.

8

Nur im Raum der Rühmung darf die Klage
gehn, die Nymphe des geweinten Quells,
wachend über unserm Niederschlage,
dass er klar sei an demselben Fels,

der die Tore trägt und die Altäre.—
Sieh, um ihre stillen Schultern früht
das Gefühl, dass sie die jüngste wäre
unter den Geschwistern im Gemüt.

Jubel *weiss*, und Sehnsucht ist geständig,—
nur die Klage lernt noch; mädchenhändig
zählt sie nächtelang das alte Schlimme.

Aber plötzlich, schräg und ungeübt,
hält sie doch ein Sternbild unsrer Stimme
in den Himmel, den ihr Hauch nicht trübt.

8

Lament, water-nymph of the wellsprings
of tears: praising's the only place
she can live—watching over our crying
to see it run clear from the rockface

that holds up our portals and altars.
Look: all round her motionless shoulders
the sense dawns that she must be youngest
of the sisters who live in our spirit.

Rejoicing *knows,* and Longing has confessed,—
only Lament is still learning: all night
she counts up old wrongs with her childish hands.

Then all at once, off-balance, out of practice,
she lifts a constellation of our voices
into the sky, undimmed by her own breath.

9

Nur wer die Leier schon hob
auch unter Schatten,
darf das unendliche Lob
ahnend erstatten.

Nur wer mit Toten vom Mohn
ass, von dem ihren,
wird nicht den leisesten Ton
wieder verlieren.

Mag auch die Spieglung im Teich
oft uns verschwimmen:
Wisse das Bild.

Erst in dem Doppelbereich
werden die Stimmen
ewig und mild.

9

You have to have been among the shades,
tuning your lyre there too,
if you want vision enough to know
how to make lasting praise.

You have to sit down and eat
with the dead, nibbling their poppies,
if you want enough memory to keep
the one most delicate note.

The image we glimpse in the pond
often grows blurred:
know it, completely.

And the world has to be twofold
before any voice can be
eternal and mild.

10

Euch, die ihr nie mein Gefühl verliesst,
grüss ich, antikische Sarkophage,
die das fröhliche Wasser römischer Tage
als ein wandelndes Lied durchfliesst.

Oder jene so offenen, wie das Aug
eines frohen erwachenden Hirten,
—innen voll Stille und Bienensaug—
denen entzückte Falter entschwirrten;

alle, die man dem Zweifel entreisst,
grüss ich, die wiedergeöffneten Munde,
die schon wussten, was schweigen heisst.

Wissen wirs, Freunde, wissen wirs nicht?
Beides bildet die zögernde Stunde
in dem menschlichen Angesicht.

10

You've never been away from me, antique
sarcophagi, but I greet you—you
whom jubilant waters have flowed through
since Roman days, as wandering music.

Or those old graves, wide open, like the eyes
of a shepherd who wakes feeling joyful,
—full of stillness and blossoming nettles—
releasing a swarm of elated butterflies;

all that we snatch away from doubt
I greet, mouths that are open once more,
having learned what silence means.

Have *we* learned that? Or have we yet
to learn? Both. Hesitating between
is what gives our faces character.

11

Sieh den Himmel. Heisst kein Sternbild „Reiter"
Denn dies ist uns seltsam eingeprägt:
dieser Stolz aus Erde. Und ein zweiter,
der ihn treibt und hält und den er trägt.

Ist nicht so, gejagt und dann gebändigt,
diese sehnige Natur des Seins?
Weg und Wendung. Doch ein Druck verständigt.
Neue Weite. Und die zwei sind eins.

Aber *sind* sie's? Oder meinen beide
nicht den Weg, den sie zusammen tun?
Namenlos schon trennt sie Tisch und Weide.

Auch die sternische Verbindung trügt.
Doch uns freue eine Weile nun,
der Figur zu glauben. Das genügt.

11

Look at the stars. Is there no constellation
called "Horseman"? For the animal's earth-pride
is strangely ingrained in us. So is the human
will to control, guide, be carried.

Isn't this chasing and being broken in
part of the sinewy nature of things?
The trail and the turn-off. Touch as understanding.
Fresh distances. And rider and horse as one.

But *are* they? Does either of them want
the path that they travel together?
Pasture and table already draw them apart.

Even that union in the stars is deceptive.
Still, let's be glad to believe in that figure
for a while now. That's enough.

12

Heil dem Geist, der uns verbinden mag;
denn wir leben wahrhaft in Figuren.
Und mit kleinen Schritten gehn die Uhren
neben unserm eigentlichen Tag.

Ohne unsern wahren Platz zu kennen,
handeln wir aus wirklichem Bezug.
Die Antennen fühlen die Antennen,
und die leere Ferne trug . . .

Reine Spannung. O Musik der Kräfte!
Ist nicht durch die lässlichen Geschäfte
jede Störung von dir abgelenkt?

Selbst wenn sich der Bauer sorgt und handelt,
wo die Saat in Sommer sich verwandelt,
reicht er niemals hin. Die Erde *schenkt*.

12

Hail to the spirit that can unite us;
for we really live only in figures.
And the clocks, with little steps, totter
alongside our actual days.

Without ever knowing our true place
we connect ourselves to what's genuine.
Antenna gropes towards antenna,
and carries the empty distance.

Pure tension. Oh music of forces!
Do our venial doings somehow
deflect what might otherwise disturb you?

The farmer can labor and fuss, but
down where the seed is changing to summer,
beyond his reach, the earth *pours out*.

13

Voller Apfel, Birne und Banane,
Stachelbeere . . . Alles dieses spricht
Tod und Leben in den Mund . . . Ich ahne . . .
Lest es einem Kind vom Angesicht,

wenn es sie erschmeckt. Dies kommt von weit.
Wird euch langsam namenlos im Munde?
Wo sonst Worte waren, fliessen Funde,
aus dem Fruchtfleisch überrascht befreit.

Wagt zu sagen, was ihr Apfel nennt.
Diese Süsse, sie sich erst verdichtet,
um, im Schmecken leise aufgerichtet,

klar zu werden, wach und transparent,
doppeldeutig, sonnig, erdig, hiesig—:
O Erfahrung, Fühlung, Freude—, riesig!

13

Ripe apple, pear and banana,
gooseberry . . . They speak of life and death
as soon as they get in our mouths . . .
Try watching a child's face: you can

see the far-off knowledge as he tastes it.
What's going on in your mouth? Something nameless,
slow. Instead of words, a flood of discoveries,
startled loose from the flesh of the fruit.

Do you dare tell what we mean by "apple"?
This sweetness that first condenses itself
so that when you lift it to take a bite

it will be pure, wide-awake, transparent,
two-meaninged, sunlike, earthlike, all presence—:
Oh experience, sensation, happiness—, *immense!*

14

Wir gehen um mit Blume, Weinblatt, Frucht.
Sie sprechen nicht die Sprache nur des Jahres.
Aus Dunkel steigt ein buntes Offenbares
und hat vielleicht den Glanz der Eifersucht

der Toten an sich, die die Erde stärken.
Was wissen wir von ihrem Teil an dem?
Es ist seit lange ihre Art, den Lehm
mit ihrem freien Marke zu durchmärken.

Nun fragt sich nur: tun sie es gern? . . .
Drängt diese Frucht, ein Werk von schweren Sklaven,
geballt zu uns empor, zu ihren Herrn?

Sind *sie* die Herrn, die bei den Wurzeln schlafen,
und gönnen uns aus ihren Überflüssen
dies Zwischending aus stummer Kraft und Küssen?

14

Always we move among flowers, vine-leaves, fruit.
They don't just speak a language of seasons.
Out of the darkness comes a motley declaration
with maybe a glimmer of jealousy in it

from the earth-nourishing dead. Do we know
what part they play in all this? Consider
just how long it has been their nature
to riddle the loam with loose bone-marrow.

This question, then: do they enjoy it?
Is fruit heaved up to us, clenched with the effort
of clumsy slaves, and we their masters?

Are *they* the masters, asleep among roots,
and grudging us from their surpluses
this crossbred thing of speechless strength and kisses?

15

Wartet . . . , das schmeckt . . . Schon ists auf der Fluch
. . . Wenig Musik nur, ein Stampfen, ein Summen—:
Mädchen, ihr warmen, Mädchen, ihr stummen,
tanzt den Geschmack der erfahrenen Frucht!

Tanzt die Orange. Wer kann sie vergessen,
wie sie, ertrinkend in sich, sich wehrt
wider ihr Süßsein. Ihr habt sie besessen.
Sie hat sich köstlich zu euch bekehrt.

Tanzt die Orange. Die wärmere Landschaft,
werft sie aus euch, dass die reife estrahle
in Lüften der Heimat! Erglühte, enthüllt

Düfte um Düfte! Schafft die Verwandschaft
mit der reinen, sich weigernden Schale,
mit dem Saft, der die glückliche füllt!

15

Wait . . . that tastes good . . . Already it's leaving.
. . . Just a faint music, a stamping, a humming—:
Girls who are warm, girls who are silent,
dance the taste of this sampled fruit!

Dance the orange. Who can forget how, drowning
in itself, it still resists the tendency
to be too sweet. Yours in possessing
it has turned into you, deliciously.

Dance the orange. Throw its warmer landscape
out of yourselves, let the ripeness shine
in its native air! Peel away, radiant,

fragrance on fragrance! Create a kinship
with the pure and reluctant rind,
with the juice that loads the ecstatic fruit!

16

Du, mein Freund, bist einsam, weil . . .
Wir machen mit Worten und Fingerzeigen
uns allmählich die Welt zu eigen,
vielleicht ihren schwächsten, gefährlichsten Teil.

Wer zeigt mit Fingern auf einen Geruch?—
Doch von den Kräften, die uns bedrohten,
fühlst du viele . . . Du kennst die Toten,
und du erschrickst vor dem Zauberspruch.

Sieh, nun heisst es zusammen ertragen
Stückwerk und Teile, als sei es das Ganze.
Dir helfen, wird schwer sein. Vor allem: pflanze

mich nicht in dein Herz. Ich wüchse zu schnell.
Doch *meines* Herrn Hand will ich führen und sagen:
Hier. Das ist Esau in seinem Fell.

16

You, my friend, are lonely, because . . .
We gradually make the world our own,
even its feeblest, riskiest portion,
with our words and pointing fingers.

Who points a finger at a smell?
Still, among the forces we dread
there are many you know . . . You sense the dead
and you cringe when you hear the magic spells.

You see, we two have to manage some way
with piecework and parts, as if they were whole.
Helping you won't be easy. Above all:

don't plant me in your heart. I'd grow too fast.
But I'll guide *my* master's hand and say:
Here: This is Esau, in his pelt.

17

Zu unterst der Alte, verworrn,
all der Erbauten
Wurzel, verborgener Born,
den sie nie schauten.

Sturmhelm und Jägerhorn,
Spruch von Ergrauten,
Männer im Bruderzorn,
Frauen wie Lauten . . .

Drängender Zweig an Zweig,
nirgends ein freier . . .
Einer! o steig . . . o steig . . .

Aber sie brechen noch.
Dieser erst oben doch
beigt sich zur Leier.

17

Deep under all that's been done,
entangled and ancient,
a hidden source, a root
no one has seen.

Hunting-horns, helmets,
words of the ancients,
men at their brother-hates,
women like lutes . . .

Branch against branch against
branch, none of them free . . .
One! Oh climb . . . climb higher . . .

Still they snap. See,
though, the top one at last
bends itself into a lyre.

18

Hörst du das Neue, Herr,
dröhnen und beben?
Kommen Verkündiger,
die es erheben.

Zwar ist kein Hören heil
in dem Durchtobtsein,
doch der Maschinenteil
will jetzt gelobt sein.

Sieh, die Maschine:
wie sie sich wälzt und rächt
und uns entstellt und schwächt.

Hat sie aus uns auch Kraft,
sie, ohne Leidenschaft,
treibe und diene.

18

Master, the New: hear it
droning and shaking?
Heralds are coming
to praise and proclaim it.

Hearing is difficult
in this new tumult,
but the machine-part
expects us to praise it.

See the machine:
with what vengeance it spins,
deforms us and shrinks us.

Though its strength comes from us,
make it dispassionate,
to drive and to serve us.

19

Wandelt sich rasch auch die Welt
wie Wolkengestalten,
alles Vollendete fällt
heim zum Uralten.

Über dem Wandel und Gang,
weiter und freier,
währt noch dein Vor-Gesang,
Gott mit der Leier.

Nicht sind die Leiden erkannt,
nicht ist die Liebe gelernt,
und was im Tod uns entfernt,

ist nicht entschleiert.
Einzig das Lied überm Land
heiligt und feiert.

19

Though this world changes
as quickly as cloud-forms,
perfections fall home
to the age-old, the ancient.

Over the changing and crowding,
wider and freer,
we still hear your primal song,
god with the lyre.

Pain is not comprehended,
love isn't truly learned.
What death erases

is never revealed.
Only the song, across the land,
hallows and praises.

20

Dir aber, Herr, o was weih ich dir, sag,
der das Ohr den Geschöpfen gelehrt?—
Mein Erinnern an einen Frühlingstag,
seinen Abend, in Russland—, ein Pferd . . .

Herüber vom Dorf kam der Schimmel allein,
an der vorderen Fessel den Pflock,
um die Nacht auf den Wiesen allein zu sein;
wie schlug seiner Mähne Gelock

an den Hals im Takte des Übermuts,
bei dem grob gehemmten Galopp.
Wie sprangen die Quellen des Rossebluts!

Der fühlte die Weiten, und ob!
der sang und der hörte—, dein Sagenkreis
war *in* ihm geschlossen.
                                        Sein Bild: ich weih's.

20

But what can I dedicate to you, Master, say,
you who taught creatures how to hear?
My memory of one spring day,
and its evening, in Russia—, a horse . . .

A white stallion that roamed in my direction
from the village, a hobble on his fetlock,
out on the meadows for the night, alone;
how the shock of his mane bounded on his neck

in time with his high spirits—and with
the rhythm of his clumsy, shackled gallop.
How the wellsprings surged, blood of the stallion!

He could feel the expanses, that one!
How he neighed, how he listened—your myth
closed its circle in him.

His image—I offer it up.

21

Frühling ist wiedergekommen. Die Erde
ist wie ein Kind, das Gedichte weiss;
viele, o viele . . . Für die Beschwerde
langen Lernens bekommt sie den Preis.

Streng war ihr Lehrer. Wir mochten das Weisse
an dem Barte des alten Manns.
Nun, wie das Grüne, das Blaue heisse,
dürfen wir fragen: sie kanns, sie kanns!

Erde, die frei hat, du glückliche, spiele
nun mit den Kindern. Wir wollen dich fangen,
fröhliche Erde. Dem Frohsten gelingts.

O, was der Lehrer sie lehrte, das Viele,
und was gedruckt steht in Wurzeln und langen
schwierigen Stämmen: sie singts, sie singts!

21

Spring's come again. The earth is
a child, full of poems she's memorized.
Many, oh many . . . If there's a prize
for that kind of learning, it's hers.

Her teacher was strict. We liked
the white in the old man's beard.
Now we can ask her the names of the blues
and the greens: always, she knows, she knows!

Earth, on vacation, happy-go-lucky, now
you can play with the children. We'll chase you,
giddy earth. And the giddiest will catch you.

What her teacher taught her!—so many things
and what is imprinted in roots and the long
intricate stems: she sings, she sings!

22

Wir sind die Treibenden.
Aber den Schritt der Zeit,
nehmt ihn als Kleinigkeit
im immer Bleibenden.

Alles das Eilende
wird schon vorüber sein;
denn das Verweilende
erst weiht uns ein.

Knaben, o werft den Mut
nicht in die Schnelligkeit,
nicht in den Flugversuch.

Alles ist ausgeruht:
Dunkel und Helligkeit,
Blume und Buch.

22

Oh how we bustle
when even Time's passing
is only a trifle
in what's everlasting.

All that's hurrying
soon will be gone;
something abiding
comes from within.

Bravery's not tested,
boys, by your swiftness,
the short flights you take.

Look to the things at rest:
darkness and brightness . . .
flower and book . . .

23

O erst *dann*, wenn der Flug
nicht mehr um seinetwillen
wird in die Himmelsstillen
steigen, sich selber genug,

um in lichten Profilen,
als das Gerät, das gelang,
Liebling der Winde zu spielen,
sicher schwenkend und schlank,—

erst wenn ein reines Wohin
wachsender Apparate
Knabenstolz überwiegt,

wird, überstürzt von Gewinn,
jener den Fernen Genahte
sein, was er einsam erfliegt.

23

Oh not until *then*, when to fly
is not for the sake of flight,
but something more self-sufficient
a rising into the silent sky—

the tool of one's own success,
to play in luminous outlines,
minion of all the winds,
slender and sure in its flourishes—

Only when a pure "where you are going?"
outweighs a boyish, still growing,
pride in machines,

will one who has brought the far near,
head over heels with succeeding,
be what only his flight was before.

24

Sollen wir unsere uralte Freundschaft, die grossen
niemals werbenden Götter, weil sie der harte
Stahl, den wir streng erzogen, nicht kennt, verstossen
oder sie plötzlich suchen auf einer Karte?

Diese gewaltigen Freunde, die uns die Toten
nehmen, rühren nirgends an unsere Räder.
Unsere Gastmähler haben wir weit—, unsere Bäder,
fortgerückt, und ihre uns lang schon zu langsamen Boten

überholen wir immer. Einsamer nun aufeinander
ganz angewiesen, ohne einander zu kennen,
führen wir nicht mehr die Pfade als schöne Mäander,

sondern als Grade. Nur noch in Dampfkesseln brennen
die einstigen Feuer und heben die Hämmer, die immer
grössern. Wir aber nehmen an Kraft ab, wie Schwimmer.

24

Must we reject our ancient friendship
with the great, undemanding gods because hard
steel hasn't touched them, steel that we've forged?
Must we suddenly look for them on a map?

These mighty friends, who take the dead from us,
don't brush against our wheels. We've set up
our baths and our banquets far off, and we outstrip
their messengers, long since too slow for us.

Lonelier now, completely dependent
on each other, not knowing each other, we don't
lay out paths that meander any more,

we make them straight. The primal fires
burn only in steam boilers now, heaving hammers
that grow stronger. While we weaken, like swimmers.

25

Dich aber will ich nun, dich, die ich kannte
wie eine Blume, von der ich den Namen nicht weiss,
noch *ein* Mal erinnern und ihnen zeigen, Entwandte,
schöne Gespielin des unüberwindlichen Schreis.

Tänzerin erst, die plötzlich, den Körper voll Zögern,
anhielt, als göss man ihr Jungsein in Erz;
trauernd und lauschend—. Da, von den hohen Vermögern
fiel ihr Musik in das veränderte Herz.

Nah war die Krankheit. Schon von den Schatten bemächtigt,
drängte verdunkelt das Blut, doch, wie flüchtig verdächtigt,
trieb es in seinen natürlichen Frühling hervor.

Wieder und wieder, von Dunkel und Sturz unterbrochen,
glänzte es irdisch. Bis es nach schrecklichem Pochen
trat in das trostlos offene Tor.

25

But you now, whom I felt like a flower
I had no name for, you, taken away,
let me show you to them *once*, let me remember,
lovely playmate, unconquerable cry.

Dancer first, who suddenly, body filled with delay,
stood still, as if her youth were being cast
in bronze. Grieving and listening. Then, from high
agents, music fell into her changing heart.

Sickness drew near. Already possessed by shadows,
her blood rushed darkening, and yet, as if running scared,
it surged toward its natural springtide.

Again and again, though falls and darkness interrupted,
it glowed like the earth. Until after hideous blows
it ran through a gate that was hopelessly wide.

26

Du aber, Göttlicher, du, bis zuletzt noch Ertöner,
da ihn der Schwarm der verschmähten Mänaden befiel,
hast ihr Geschrei übertönt mit Ordnung, du Schöner,
aus den Zerstörenden stieg dein erbauendes Spiel.

Keine war da, dass sie Haupt dir und Leier zerstör',
wie sie auch rangen und rasten; und alle die scharfen
Steine, die sie nach deinem Herzen warfen,
wurden zu Sanftem an dir und begabt mit Gehör.

Schliesslich zerschlugen sie dich, von der Rache gehetzt,
während dein Klang noch in Löwen und Felsen verweilte
und in den Bäumen und Vögeln. Dort singst du noch jetzt.

O du verlorener Gott! Du unendliche Spur!
Nur weil dich reissend zuletzt die Feindschaft verteilte,
sind wir die Hörenden jetzt und ein Mund der Natur.

26

But you, godlike, beautiful—when the horde
of scorned Maenads attacked, you went on sounding,
right to the end; drowning their cries with order,
up from that mayhem rose your building song.

They couldn't break your lyre or your head,
however they tried, wrestling and raging;
and the sharp stones they threw at your heart turned
soft against you, and capable of hearing.

They tore you to pieces at last, in a frenzy,
while your sound lingered on in lions and rocks,
and in trees and birds. You still sing there.

Oh you lost god! You everlasting trace! Only
because that hatred ripped and scattered you
are we listeners now, and one mouth of Nature.

SECOND PART

1

Atmen, du unsichtbares Gedicht!
Immerfort um das eigne
Sein rein eingetauschter Weltraum. Gegengewicht,
in dem ich mich rhythmisch ereigne.

Einzige Welle, deren
allmähliches Meer ich bin;
sparsamstes du von allen möglichen Meeren,—
Raumgewinn.

Wie viele von diesen Stellen der Raüme waren schon
innen in mir. Manche Winde
sind wie mein Sohn.

Erkennst du mich, Luft, du, voll noch einst meiniger Orte?
Du, einmal glatte Rinde,
Rundung und Blatt meiner Worte.

1

Breathing, you invisible poem!
Worldspace incessantly having its pure
traffic with our own being. Counterweight system
in which I rhythmically occur.

Lone wave, whose
gradual sea I am;
you sparsest of possible seas—
making room.

How many places in space have already
been inside me! Many a wind
is like a son to me . . .

Do you know me, air? You, full of places which
once were mine? You—once the smooth rind,
the roundness and leaf of my speech.

2

So wie dem Meister manchmal das eilig
nähere Blatt den *wirklichen* Strich
abnimmt: so nehmen oft Spiegel das heilig
einzige Lächeln der Mädchen in sich,

wenn sie den Morgen erproben, allein,—
oder im Glanze der dienenden Lichter.
Und in das Atmen der echten Gesichter,
später, fällt nur ein Widerschein.

Was haben Augen einst ins umrusste
lange Verglühn der Kamine geschaut:
Blicke des Lebens, für immer verlorne.

Ach, der Erde, wer kennt die Verluste?
Nur, wer mit dennoch preisendem Laut
sänge das Herz, das ins Ganze geborne.

2

As the snatched paper, nearest to hand,
sometimes captures the Master's *true* stroke,
so mirrors, often, absorb the holy
solitary smiles of young women: when

they test the morning, alone—or in
the glow served up as lamps and candles burn.
What returns to the breathing and genuine
faces, later, is merely a stale reflection.

What happens, then, when eyes have gazed
at the slow, charred glowing of the fireplace?
Life-glances, lost forever.

The earth! Who knows about her losses? Whoever
can sing of the heart, whoever can still praise,
born into such a place.

3

Spiegel: noch nie hat man wissend beschrieben,
was ihr in euerem Wesen seid.
Ihr, wie mit lauter Löchern von Sieben
erfüllten Zwischenräume der Zeit.

Ihr, noch des leeren Saales Verschwender—,
wenn es dämmert, wie Wälder weit . . .
Und der Lüster geht wie ein Sechzehn-Ender
durch eure Unbetretbarkeit.

Manchmal seid ihr voll Malerei.
Einige scheinen *in* euch gegangen—,
andere schicktet ihr scheu vorbei.

Aber die Schönste wird bleiben, bis
drüben in ihre enthaltenen Wangen
eindrang der klare gelöste Narziss.

3

Mirrors: no one who knows has ever
described you, said what you're really like.
You who are filled with gaps of time
the way holes fill a sieve.

Spendthrifts in empty drawing rooms,
when evening arrives, deep as the woods . . .
like a sixteen-point stag, the faint shine roams
through your unreachable solitudes.

At times you seem filled with paintings.
Some seem to go straight into you—others
you've shyly sent away. Of course

the loveliest one will remain, until
there in those self-contained cheeks, clear
Narcissus, released, breaks in by force.

4

O dieses ist das Tier, das es nicht gibt.
Sie wusstens nicht und habens jeden Falls
—sein Wandeln, seine Haltung, seinen Hals,
bis in des stillen Blickes Licht—geliebt.

Zwar *war* es nicht. Doch weil sie's liebten, ward
ein reines Tier. Sie liessen immer Raum.
Und in dem Raume, klar und ausgespart,
erhob es leicht sein Haupt und brauchte kaum

zu sein. Sie nährten es mit keinem Korn,
nur immer mit der Möglichkeit, es sei.
Und sie gab solche Stärke an das Tier,

dass es aus sich ein Stirnhorn trieb. Ein Horn.
Zu einer Jungfrau kam es weiss herbei—
und war im Silber-Spiegel und in ihr.

4

Oh this is the animal that never was.
They didn't know that, they just went ahead
and loved it; its walk, bearing, neck—they loved
even the light of its silent gaze.

Never existed. And yet, because they loved,
a pure creature began to occur. They always
left room for it, and in that cleared space
it simply lifted its head, and hardly needed

to exist. They never fed it grain
but rather, always, possibility.
And that gave the animal such energy

that it grew a brow-horn. A single horn.
And it came white unto a virgin here—
and *was,* in the silver mirror, and in her.

5

Blumenmuskel, der der Anemone
Wiesenmorgen nach und nach erschliesst,
bis in ihren Schooss das polyphone
Licht der lauten Himmel sich ergiesst,

in den stillen Blütenstern gespannter
Muskel des unendlichen Empfangs,
manchmal *so* von Fülle übermannter,
dass der Ruhewink des Untergangs

kaum vermag die weitzurückgeschnellten
Blätterränder dir zurückzugeben:
du, Entschluss und Kraft von *wieviel* Welten!

Wir Gewaltsamen, wir währen länger.
Aber *wann,* in welchem aller Leben,
sind wir endlich offen und Empfänger?

5

Flower-muscle, that unlocks, bit by bit,
the meadow-morning of the anemone,
until the polyphonic sky's loud light
pours down into her lap,

muscle of endless receptiveness
stretched in the quiet blossom-star,
so overcome, sometimes, by fullness,
that sundown's signal to rest

barely allows you to refurl
the overextended petals: you, the drive
and energy of how many worlds!

We violent ones last longer.
But *when,* in which of all our lives,
are we so open, such receivers?

6

Rose, du thronende, denen im Altertume
warst du ein Kelch mit einfachem Rand.
Uns aber bist du die volle zahllose Blume,
der unerschöpfliche Gegenstand.

In deinem Reichtum scheinst due wie Kleidung um Kleidung
um einen Leib aus nichts als Glanz;
aber dein einzelnes Blatt ist zugleich die Vermeidung
und die Verleugnung jedes Gewands.

Seit Jahrhunderten ruft uns dein Duft
seine süssesten Namen herüber;
plötzlich liegt er wie Ruhm in der Luft.

Dennoch, wir wissen ihn nicht zu nennen, wir raten . . .
Und Erinnerung geht zu ihm über,
die wir von rufbaren Stunden erbaten.

6

Rose, growing throne of yourself, to the ancients
you were a chalice with a simple rim.
For us you're the full, innumerable bloom,
the inexhaustible subject.

In your opulence you seem like clothing around clothing
around a body that's nothing more than brightness;
but your separate leaf is both the shunning
and the denial of every kind of dress.

For centuries your fragrance called across
its sweetest names to us; it's there
suddenly, hanging in the air like fame.

Still, we don't know what to call it. We guess . . .
and memory, summoned from hours we *could* name,
gives itself up to that fragrance once more.

7

Blumen, ihr schliesslich den ordnenden Händen verwandte,
(Händen der Mädchen von einst und jetzt),
die auf dem Gartentische oft von Kante zu Kante
lagen, ermattet und sanft verletzt,

wartend des Wassers, das sie noch einmal erhole
aus dem begonnenen Tod—, und nun
wieder erhobene zwischen die strömenden Pole
fühlender Finger, die wohlzutun

mehr noch vermögen, als ihr ahntet, ihr leichten,
wenn ihr euch wiederfandet im Krug,
langsam erkühlend und Warmes von Mädchen, wie Beichten,

von euch gebend, wie trübe ermüdende Sünden,
die das Gepflücktsein beging, als Bezug
wieder zu ihnen, die sich euch blühend verbünden.

7

Flowers, kinfolk at last to arranging hands,
(hands of young women, long ago and now), you
who lay on the garden table, often from rim to
rim, weary and mildly wounded

awaiting the water that would revive you
from death, already begun—, and now
lifted again between the streaming poles
of feeling fingers, that have even more power

to do good that you guessed, weightless ones,
when you came to in the jug, cooling slowly
and giving off the warmth of young women

like confessions, like thick, fatiguing sins
the act of plucking brought on, relating you again
to those who ally themselves with your blooming.

8

Wenige ihr, der einstigen Kindheit Gespielen
in den zerstreuten Gärten der Stadt:
wie wir uns fanden und uns zögernd gefielen
und, wie das Lamm mit dem redenden Blatt,

sprachen als schweigende. Wenn wir uns einmal freuten,
keinem gehörte es. Wessen wars?
Und wie zergings unter allen den gehenden Leuten
und im Bangen des langen Jahrs.

Wagen umrollten uns fremd, vorübergezogen,
Häuser umstanden uns stark, aber unwahr,—und keines
kannte uns je. *Was* war wirklich im All?

Nichts. Nur die Bälle. Ihre herrlichen Bogen.
Auch nicht die Kinder . . . Aber manchmal trat eines,
ach ein vergehendes, unter den fallenden Ball.

In memoriam Egon von Rilke

8

You few, you playmates of time and time ago,
there in the scattered gardens of the town:
how we found each other, gingerly made friends,
and, like the lamb with the talking scroll,

spoke silently. If we happened to please each other
nobody owned that. Whose would it be?
And how it melted among the passers-by
and vanished among the fears of the long year.

Carriages rolled around us, drawn along unperturbed,
houses stood round us, strong but unreal—and nothing
ever recognized us. What in this world *was* real?

Nothing. Only the balls. Their magnificent curves.
Not even the children . . . But sometimes one would step,
oh little vanishing thing, under the falling ball.

In memoriam Egon von Rilke

9

Rühmt euch, ihr Richtenden, nicht der entbehrlichen Folter
und dass das Eisen nicht länger an Hälsen sperrt.
Keins ist gesteigert, kein Herz—, weil ein gewollter
Krampf der Milde euch zarter verzerrt.

Was es durch Zeiten bekam, das schenkt das Schafott
wieder zurück, wie Kinder ihr Spielzeug vom vorig
alten Geburtstag. Ins reine, ins hohe, ins torig
offene Herz träte er anders, der Gott

wirklicher Milde. Er käme gewaltig und griffe
strahlender um sich, wie Göttliche sind.
Mehr als ein Wind für die grossen gesicherten Schiffe.

Weniger nicht, als die heimliche leise Gewahrung,
die uns im Innern schweigend gewinnt
wie ein still spielendes Kind aus unendlicher Paarung.

9

So you've abandoned torture? And the iron chains
that used to shackle necks? Justicers, don't boast.
Not one neck is raised, not one heart, because some ordained
cramp of mercy gave you a mild twist.

The scaffold will give back what time has given it
as children do playthings left from old
birthdays. Into the pure, into the high, into the heart
swung wide like gates, he'd enter differently, the god

of genuine mercy. He would come forcefully, he'd grip
those around him with radiance, the way of the godlike.
More than a wind for the giant, unshakable ships.

And not less than the fine and private feeling
that conquers us silently from within, like
the child of an infinite coupling, quietly playing.

10

Alles Erworbne bedroht die Maschine, solange
sie sich endreistet, im Geist, statt im Gehorchen, zu sein.
Dass nicht der herrlichen Hand schöneres Zögern
                                        mehr prange,
zu dem entschlossenern Bau schneidet sie steifer den Stein.

Nirgends bleibt sie zurück, dass wir ihr *ein* Mal entrönnen
und sie in stiller Fabrik ölend sich selber gehört.
Sie ist das Leben,—sie meint es am besten zu können,
die mit dem gleichen Entschluss ordnet und schafft und zerstört.

Aber noch ist uns das Dasein verzaubert; an hundert
Stellen ist es noch Ursprung. Ein Spielen von reinen
Kräften, die keiner berührt, der nicht kniet und bewundert.

Worte gehen noch zart am Unsäglichen aus . . .
Und die Musik, immer neu, aus den bebendsten Steinen,
baut im unbrauchbaren Raum ihr vergöttlichtes Haus.

10

The machine: as long as it disobeys, and dares
to exist in the spirit, it threatens all we've won.
Against the fine shows of the hand
                                      those sweet hesitations
it cuts the harsh building's stones to be even more severe.

It never stays back where for once we could just
leave it behind, oiling itself in the shut factory.
It is life—it thinks it does everything best,
with the same calm resolve to regulate, make and destroy.

But existence can still enchant us; in a hundred
places, we find its wells and springs. A play of pure forces
that no one can touch without wanting to kneel in wonder.

Words still fail softly before the unsayable . . .
And music, always new, builds in unusable space
and out of the shakiest stones, her holiest house.

11

Manche, des Todes, entstand ruhig geordnete Regel,
weiterbezwingender Mensch, seit du im Jagen beharrst;
mehr doch als Falle und Netz, weiss ich dich, Streifen von Segel,
den man hinuntergehängt in den höhligen Karst.

Leise liess man dich ein, als wärst du ein Zeichen,
Frieden zu feiern. Doch dann: rang dich am Rande der Knecht,
—und, aus den Höhlen, die Nacht warf eine Handvoll von
   bleichen
taumelnden Tauben ins Licht . . . Aber auch *das* ist im Recht.

Fern von dem Schauenden sei jeglicher Hauch des Bedauerns,
nicht *nur* vom Jäger allein, der, was sich zeitig erweist,
wachsam und handelnd vollzieht.

Töten ist eine Gestalt unseres wandernden Trauerns . . .
Rein ist im heiteren Geist,
was an uns geschieht.

11

Many a rule for death has been calmly set up
since we started to hunt, we who must conquer further;
yet better than any net or trap I know *you,* canvas strip,
that they used to let down into the Carso caverns.

They'd lower you gently, as if you were some signal
in honor of peace. But then: the farmhand gave you a twitch
—and out of the caves Night tossed a bleached handful
of giddy doves to the light . . . But even *that* is all right.

Let no gasp of pity be heard from the witness
any more than the hunter, who does as he must, alert
and ready to act when the moment is right.

Killing is one form of our wandering sadness . . .
Whatever has happened to us
is pure in the radiant spirit.

12

Wolle die Wandlung. O sei für die Flamme begeistert,
drin sich ein Ding dir entzieht, das mit Verwandlungen prunkt;
jener entwerfende Geist, welcher das Irdische meistert,
liebt in dem Schwung der Figur nichts wie den wendenden
    Punkt.

Was sich ins Bleiben verschliesst, schon *ists* das Erstarrte;
wähnt es sich sicher im Schutz des unscheinbaren Grau's?
Warte, ein Härtestes warnt aus der Ferne das Harte.
Wehe—: abwesender Hammer holt aus!

Wer sich als Quelle ergiesst, den erkennt die Erkennung;
und sie führt ihn entzückt durch das heiter Geschaffne,
das mit Anfang oft schliesst und mit Ende beginnt.

Jeder glückliche Raum ist Kind oder Enkel von Trennung,
den sie staunend durchgehn. Und die verwandelte Daphne
will, seit sie lorbeern fühlt, dass du dich wandelst in Wind.

12

You must *wish* for change. Be rapt for the flame wherein
a thing eludes you, gaudy with flux; the spirit
that mastered the earthly by tracing its outlines
loves most in the figure's swing the rotating point.

What shuts itself up in staying is already rigid;
does it think itself safe in the shelter of nondescript gray?
Wait: from a distance the hardest is warning the hard.
Watch out—, an absent hammer is raised!

He who pours himself out like a spring—Perception perceives
    him,
and leads him, delighted, through brilliant regions and realms
that end with beginnings, and often with endings begin.

Each happy space they traverse, amazed, is a child
or grandchild of parting. And ever since she felt laurel-like,
Daphne, transformed, has wished you would change yourself to
    wind.

13

Sei allem Abschied voran, als wäre er hinter
dir, wie der Winter, der eben geht.
Denn unter Wintern ist einer so endlos Winter,
dass, überwinternd, dein Herz überhaupt übersteht.

Sei immer tot in Eurydike—, singender steige,
preisender steige zurück in den reinen Bezug.
Hier, unter Schwindenden, sei, im Reiche der Neige,
sei ein klingendes Glas, das sich im Klang schon zerschlug.

Sei—und wisse zugleich des Nicht-Seins Bedingung,
den unendlichen Grund deiner innigen Schwingung,
dass du sie völlig vollziehst dieses einzige Mal.

Zu dem gebrauchten sowohl, wie zum dumpfen und stummen
Vorrat der vollen Natur, den unsäglichen Summen,
zähle dich jubelnd hinzu und vernichte die Zahl.

13

Be ahead of all partings, as if they were
behind you, like the winter that's just past.
For among the winters is one so endlessly winter
that your heart, if you overwinter, can survive it.

Be dead in Eurydice, always—, climb with more song,
climb with more praise, back up into pure relation.
Here in the kingdom of decay, among what's wasting,
be a tingling glass that shatters itself with sound.

Exist while you know the state of nonexistence,
the endless ground of your own deep pulse, so that
you can fulfill it completely this one time.

With the used-up, as well as the muffled and useless
stock of full nature, the unreckoned sum,
count yourself in, rejoicing, and then demolish the count.

14

Siehe die Blumen, diese dem Irdischen treuen,
denen wir Schicksal vom Rande des Schicksals leihn,—
aber wer weiss es! Wenn sie ihr Welken bereuen,
ist es an uns, ihre Reue zu sein.

Alles will schweben. Da gehn wir umher wie Beschwerer,
legen auf alles uns selbst, vom Gewichte entzückt;
o was sind wir den Dingen für zehrende Lehrer,
weil ihnen ewige Kindheit glückt.

Nähme sie einer ins innige Schlafen und schliefe
tief mit den Dingen—: o wie käme er leicht,
anders zum anderen Tag, aus der gemeinsamen Tiefe.

Oder er bliebe vielleicht; und sie blühten und priesen
ihn, den Bekehrten, der nun den Ihrigen gleicht,
allen den stillen Geschwistern im Winde der Wiesen.

14

Look at the flowers, loyal to the earth—
we lend them fate from fate's border, but
who knows if they regret the way they wither?
Maybe it's we who are their real regret.

All things want to float. And we go around like burdens,
settling ourselves on everything, ravished by weight;
what deadly teachers we are, when things in fact
have the gift of forever being children.

If someone took them into inmost sleep and slept
soundly with things—how lightly he might rise
changed, to changed days, from that communal depth.

Or maybe he'd stay; and they'd blossom and praise
him, the convert, now one with those brothers and sisters
all still in the midst of the winds and the meadows.

15

O Brunnen-Mund, du gebender, du Mund,
der unerschöpflich Eines, Reines, spricht,—
du, vor des Wassers fliessendem Gesicht,
marmorne Maske. Und im Hintergrund

der Aquädukte Herkunft. Weither an
Gräbern vorbei, vom Hang des Apennins
tragen sie dir dein Sagen zu, das dann
am schwarzen Altern deines Kinns

vorüberfällt in das Gefäss davor.
Dies ist das schlafend hingelegte Ohr,
das Marmor-Ohr, in das du immer sprichst.

Ein Ohr der Erde. Nur mit sich allein
redet sie also. Schiebt ein Krug sich ein,
so scheint es ihr, dass du sie unterbrichst.

15

Oh fountain-mouth, giver, you never-tiring
mouth that says and says the same pure thing—
you marble mask, held up against
the water's streaming face. And in the distances

the aqueducts' descent. From far away,
from the Apennine slopes, passing graves,
they carry you your speech, which then
spills down the aging blackness of your chin

and falls into the basin there.
Basin: the sleeping, sidelong ear,
the marble ear in which you always speak.

One of the earth's ears. So that she's talking
just to herself. Push a pitcher in between,
she'll think you're interrupting.

16

Immer wieder von uns aufgerissen,
ist der Gott die Stelle, welche heilt.
Wir sind Scharfe, denn wir wollen wissen,
aber er ist heiter und verteilt.

Selbst die reine, die geweihte Spende
nimmt er anders nicht in seine Welt,
als indem er sich dem freien Ende
unbewegt entgegenstellt.

Nur der Tote trinkt
aus der hier von uns *gehörten* Quelle,
wenn der Gott ihm schweigend winkt, dem Toten.

Uns wird nur das Lärmen angeboten.
Und das Lamm erbittet seine Schelle
aus dem stilleren Instinkt.

16

The place we rip open again and again
that always heals—that's God.
We are all sharp-edged from our need
to know; He is spread out, serene.

Even the pure and blessed libations
He takes into His world in just
one way: by staying motionless,
never controlling the way things turn out.

Only the dead drink
from that spring that we can *hear,*
when the god signals to them, silently.

Just the noise of it reaches us.
And the lamb begs for its bell
out of its quieter instinct.

17

Wo, in welchen immer selig bewässerten Gärten, an welchen
Bäumen, aus welchen zärtlich entblätterten Blüten-Kelchen
reifen die fremdartigen Früchte der Tröstung? Diese
köstlichen, deren du eine vielleicht in der zertretenen Wiese

deiner Armut findest. Von einem zum anderen Male
wunderst du dich über die Grösse der Frucht,
über ihr Heilsein, über die Sanftheit der Schale,
und dass sie der Leichtsinn des Vogels dir nicht vorwegnahm
                                        und nicht die Eifersucht

unten des Wurms. Gibt es denn Bäume, von Engeln beflogen,
und von verborgenen langsamen Gärtnern so seltsam gezogen,
dass sie uns tragen, ohne uns zu gehören?

Haben wir niemals vermocht, wir Schatten und Schemen,
durch unser voreilig reifes und wieder welkes Benehmen
jener gelassenen Sommer Gleichmut zu stören?

17

In what watered, ever-blissful gardens? On what trees?
From what flower-goblets, gently stripped of petals,
do these exotic fruits of consolation ripen? These
luscious fruits—you might find one in the trampled

meadow of your loss. And time and time again
you wonder: at the size of the fruit, its firm
well-being, the smoothness of its skin, and then
that some quick bird didn't beat you to it, or a worm

come jealous from below. Are trees, then,
angel-visited, strangely raised by slow and hidden
gardeners, that bear for us though we don't own them?

Haven't we ever been able, we shadows, we phantoms,
by our ripe-too-soon and withering behavior,
to shatter the calm of unruffled summer?

18

Tänzerin: o du Verlegung
alles Vergehens in Gang: wie brachtest du's dar.
Und der Wirbel am Schluss, dieser Baum aus Bewegung,
nahm er nicht ganz in Besitz das erschwungene Jahr?

Blühte nicht, dass ihn dein Schwingen von vorhin umschwärme,
plötzlich sein Wipfel von Stille? Und über ihr,
war sie nicht Sonne, war sie nicht Sommer, die Wärme,
diese unzählige Wärme aus dir?

Aber er trug auch, er trug, dein Baum der Ekstase.
Sind sie nicht seine ruhigen Früchte: der Krug,
reifend gestreift, und die gereiftere Vase?

Und in den Bildern: ist nicht die Zeichnung geblieben,
die deiner Braue dunkler Zug
rasch an die Wandung der eigenen Wendung geschrieben?

18

Dancer: oh you relaying of every
vanishing into a stride: how you performed it there!
And the twirl at the finish, that tree made of energy,
didn't it fully capture the swing of the year?

Didn't that tree's crown suddenly blossom with quiet
so your whirling could swarm up around it? And over you
wasn't it sun, wasn't it summer, the warmth of it,
this immeasurable warmth, coming from you?

But it bore too, it bore, your tree of ecstasy.
What are these but its tranquil fruits: the pitcher,
streaked with its ripening, the even riper vase.

And in the pictures: the sketch
that your eyebrow's dark stroke made
on the wall of its own swift turn—didn't it stay?

19

Irgendwo wohnt das Gold in der verwöhnenden Bank,
und mit Tausenden tut es vertraulich. Doch jener
Blinde, der Bettler, ist selbst dem kupfernen Zehner
wie ein verlorener Ort, wie das staubige Eck unterm Schrank.

In den Geschäften entlang ist das Geld wie zu Hause
und verkleidet sich scheinbar in Seide, Nelken und Pelz.
Er, der Schweigende, steht in der Atempause
alles des wach oder schlafend atmenden Gelds.

O wie mag sie sich schliessen bei Nacht, diese immer offene
    Hand.
Morgen holt sie das Schicksal wieder, und täglich
hält es sie hin: hell, elend, unendlich zerstörbar.

Dass doch einer, ein Schauender, endlich ihren langen Bestand
staunend begriffe und rühmte. Nur dem Aufsingenden säglich.
Nur dem Göttlichen hörbar.

19

Somewhere, coddled in the bank, gold lives,
chummy with thousands. But this blindman, this beggar:
even to copper pennies he's a lost place, he's
the dusty corner underneath the dresser.

Money's at home in all the shops—has many
ways to dress: silks, carnations, furs. In the pause
between each breath the silent beggar stands,
while it wakes and sleeps, all that breathing money.

Oh how does it close at night, that always open hand?
Fate brings it back each day and holds it out:
glowing, miserable, endlessly asking for hurt.

If only some witness would finally, in wonder,
grasp its persistence and praise it. Sayable just to the singer.
Audible just to the god.

20

Zwischen den Sternen, wie weit; und doch, um wievieles
$\qquad$ noch weiter,
was man am Hiesigen lernt.
Einer, zum Beispiel, ein Kind . . . und ein Nächster,
$\qquad$ ein Zweiter—,
o wie unfasslich entfernt.

Schicksal, es misst uns vielleicht mit des Seienden Spanne,
dass es uns fremd erscheint;
denk, wieviel Spannen allein vom Mädchen zum Manne,
wenn es ihn meidet und meint.

Alles ist weit—, und nirgends schliesst sich der Kreis.
Sieh in der Schüssel, auf heiter bereitetem Tische,
seltsam der Fische Gesicht.

Fische sind stumm . . . , meinte man einmal. Wer weiss?
Aber ist nicht am Ende ein Ort, wo man das, was der Fische
Sprache wäre, *ohne* sie spricht?

20

From star to star: how far that is! Yet how much farther
the things we learn from near at hand.
Some person, a child for instance . . . then next to him, another—
an unbelievable distance.

Maybe Fate measures us in being-spaces
and that's what seems so strange; consider
how many such spaces from a woman to a man
when she avoids him and at the same time *cares*.

Everything's distant—, and the circle doesn't close.
On the gaily set table, there on that platter,
look: the strange faces of fish.

Fish are dumb . . . so we thought. Who knows?
Is there a place where, even in their absence,
we can speak the language of fish?

21

Singe die Gaïten, mein Herz, die du nicht kennst; wie in Glas
eingegossene Gärten, klar, unerreichbar.
Wasser und Rosen von Ispahan oder Schiras,
singe sie selig, preise sie, keinem vergleichbar.

Zeige, mein Herz, dass du sie niemals entbehrst.
Dass sie dich meinen, ihre reifenden Feigen.
Dass du mit ihren, zwischen den blühenden Zweigen
wie zum Gesicht gesteigerten Lüften verkehrst.

Meide den Irrtum, dass es Entbehrungen gebe
für den geschehnen Entschluss, diesen: zu sein!
Seidener Faden, kamst du hinein ins Gewebe.

Welchem der Bilder du auch im Innern geeint bist
(sei es selbst ein Moment aus dem Leben der Pein),
fühl, dass der ganze, der rühmliche Teppich gemeint ist.

21

Sing the gardens, my heart, that you don't know; gardens
like those poured in glass, clear, unattainable.
Water and roses of Isfahan, Shiraz,
sing them happily, praise them, call them incomparable.

Show, heart, that you don't miss them, show
how they have you in mind as they ripen their figs;
how you hobnob with breezes that almost grow
visible there, among blossoming twigs.

Shun the error of thinking you've missed something,
because a resolve, once taken, means: to be!
Silk thread—you went into the weaving.

Whatever picture you may be inwardly part of
(even a moment in Pain's biography),
feel that what's meant is the whole splendid carpet.

22

O trotz Schicksal: die herrlichen Überflüsse
unseres Daseins, in Parken übergeschäumt,—
oder als steinerne Männer neben die Schlüsse
hoher Portale, unter Balkone gebäumt!

O die eherne Glocke, die ihre Keule
täglich wider den stumpfen Alltag hebt.
Oder die *eine,* in Karnak, die Säule, die Säule,
die fast ewige Tempel überlebt.

Heute stürzen die Überschüsse, dieselben,
nur noch als Eile vorbei, aus dem wagrechten gelben
Tag in die blendend mit Licht übertriebene Nacht.

Aber das Rasen zergeht und lässt keine Spuren.
Kurven des Flugs durch die Luft und die, die sie fuhren,
keine vielleicht ist umsonst. Doch nur wie gedacht.

22

Oh but in spite of Fate: the marvelous overflows
of our existence, foaming up into parks,—or as
stone men, flanking the keystones
of high portals, rearing up under balconies!

Oh the brazen bell, that swings its bludgeon
daily against the workaday and commonplace.
Or the *one* in Karnak, the column, the column,
that outlasts the almost eternal temples.

Today the overspills plunge by, the same ones,
but only as haste, out of the level yellow day
into a night blinding with magnified light.

But the frenzy passes and leaves no traces.
Flightcurves through air and those who rode them away,
none, maybe, is useless. Yet only as thought.

23

Rufe mich zu jener deiner Stunden,
die dir unaufhörlich widersteht:
flehend nah wie das Gesicht von Hunden,
aber immer wieder weggedreht,

wenn du meinst, sie endlich zu erfassen.
So Entzognes ist am meisten dein.
Wir sind frei. Wir wurden dort entlassen,
wo wir meinten, erst begrüsst zu sein.

Bang verlangen wir nach einem Halte,
wir zu Jungen manchmal für das Alte
und zu alt für das, was niemals war.

Wir, gerecht nur, wo wir dennoch preisen,
weil wir, der Ast sind und das Eisen
und das Süsse reifender Gefahr.

23

Of all your hours, call me to the one
that constantly resists you: close
as a dog's imploring face,
but always turning away again

just when you think you've grasped it.
What's withdrawn that way is what's most yours.
We are free. There, where we thought we were
welcome, that's where we were dismissed.

Fearful, we call for a handhold;
sometimes we're too young for what is old
and too old for what never was,

we who do justice only when we can praise
because we are the branch and we are the steel
and the sweetness of ripening trouble.

24

O diese Lust, immer neu, aus gelockertem Lehm!
Niemand beinah hat den frühesten Wagern geholfen.
Städte entstanden trotzdem an beseligten Golfen,
Wasser und Öl füllten die Krüge trotzdem.

Götter, wir planen sie erst in erkühnten Entwürfen,
die uns das mürrische Schicksal wieder zerstört.
Aber sie sind die Unsterblichen. Sehet, wir dürfen
jenen erhorchen, der uns am Ende erhört.

Wir, ein Geschlecht durch Jahrtausende: Mütter und Väter,
immer erfüllter von dem künftigen Kind,
dass es uns einst, übersteigend, erschüttere, später.

Wir, wir unendlich Gewagten, was haben wir Zeit!
Und nur der schweigsame Tod, der weiss, was wir sind
und was er immer gewinnt, wenn er uns leiht.

24

This delight, always fresh, in the loosening of soil!
The earliest risk-takers—almost no one helped them.
But cities rose up by blissful gulfs all the same,
pitchers filled, all the same, with water, with oil.

Gods—first we sketch them in daring designs
that surly Fate tears up for us again.
But they are the immortals. Look, we can
hear those out who will hear us at the end.

We're thousand-year generations: mothers and fathers,
filled more and more with the child of the future
so that someday, climbing over, it can convulse us.

We're the endlessly risked ones; what time-spans are ours!
And only tight-lipped Death knows what we really are
and what he always gets from the way he lends us.

25

Schon, horch, hörst du der ersten Harken
Arbeit; wieder den menschlichen Takt
in der verhaltenen Stille der starken
Vorfrühlingserde. Unabgeschmackt

scheint dir das Kommende. Jenes so oft
dir schon Gekommene scheint dir zu kommen
wieder wie Neues. Immer erhofft,
nahmst du es niemals. Es hat dich genommen.

Selbst die Blätter durchwinterter Eichen
scheinen im Abend ein künftiges Braun.
Manchmal geben sich Lüfte ein Zeichen.

Schwarz sind die Sträucher. Doch Haufen von Dünger
lagern als satteres Schwarz in den Au'n.
Jede Stunde, die hingeht, wird jünger.

25

Listen. You can hear harrows at work,
the first ones. Again, the human rhythms
in the hanging stillness of the rank
early-spring earth. What's coming seems

untasted, completely new. What
came to you so often seems now to
come the first time. You always expected it,
but you never took it. It took you.

Even leaves that hung on the oaks all winter
seem, in the evening, to be a future brown.
Sometimes the winds pass a signal around.

The thickets are black. But heaps of manure
are an even darker black in the pastures.
Every hour that goes by is younger.

26

Wie ergreift uns der Vogelschrei . . .
Irgendein einmal erschaffenes Schreien.
Aber die Kinder schon, spielend im Freien,
schreien an wirklichen Schreien vorbei.

Schreien den Zufall. In Zwischenräume
dieses, des Weltraums, (in welchen der heile
Vogelschrei eingeht, wie Menschen in Träume—)
treiben sie ihre, des Kreischens, Keile.

Wehe, wo sind wir? Immer noch freier,
wie die losgerissenen Drachen
jagen wir halbhoch, mit Rändern von Lachen,

windig zerfetzten.—Ordne die Schreier,
singender Gott! dass sie rauschend erwachen,
tragend als Strömung das Haupt und die Leier.

26

How a bird's cry can move us . . .
Any cry, once made.
But the children, playing outside,
already cry beyond real cries.

Cry about chance. Into gaps that occur
in this world-space (gaps where the pure
birdcry slips through, as we slip into dreams—)
they drive their thin wedges of scream.

Alas, where are we? Always freer,
like kites broken loose and scattered,
we chase through mid-air, laughter-fringed,

wind-tattered,—Arrange these criers,
singing god! that they waken and thunder together,
a current to carry the head and the lyre.

27

Gibt es wirklich die Zeit, die zerstörende?
Wann, auf dem ruhenden Berg, zerbricht sie die Burg?
Dieses Herz, das unendlich den Göttern gehörende,
wann vergewaltigts der Demiurg?

Sind wir wirklich so ängstlich Zerbrechliche,
wie das Schicksal uns wahrmachen will?
Ist die Kindheit, die tiefe, versprechliche,
in den Wurzeln—später—still?

Ach, das Gespenst des Vergänglichen,
durch den arglos Empfänglichen
geht es, als wär es ein Rauch.

Als die, die wir sind, als die Treibenden,
gelten wir doch bei bleibenden
Kräften als göttlicher Brauch.

27

Does Time, the destroyer, really exist?
Will it crumble the castle on the mountain there?
And when will the Demiurge assault this heart
that belongs to the gods forever?

Are we really as anxiously breakable
as Fate wants us to think? Can it be that
childhood, so deep, so promiseful,
is killed, later on, at the root?

Ah, the phantom of evanescence—
it goes right through the innocent,
the susceptible, as though it were vapor.

Whatever we are, driving and driven,
we matter, still, among lasting powers,
as one of the habits gods have.

28

O komm und geh. Du, fast noch Kind, ergänze
für einen Augenblick die Tanzfigur
zum reinen Sternbild eines jener Tänze,
darin wir die dumpf ordnende Natur

vergänglich übertreffen. Denn sie regte
sich völlig hörend nur, da Orpheus sang.
Du warst noch die von damals her Bewegte
und leicht befremdet, wenn ein Baum sich lang

besann, mit dir nach dem Gehör zu gehn.
Du wusstest noch die Stelle, wo die Leier
sich tönend hob—; die unerhörte Mitte.

Für sie versuchtest du die schönen Schritte
und hofftest, einmal zu der heilen Feier
des Freundes Gang und Antlitz hinzudrehn.

28

Oh come and go. Half-child, dance out the whole
figure for a moment, complete it, a pure
star-pattern, one of those dances where
we momentarily excel

Nature's sluggish order. For she only roused herself
to full attention, listening, when Orpheus sang.
You were still moved by that event, far-off,
and a little surprised if a tree took too long

deciding to go along with you to hear.
You still knew the place where the lyre
rose through its own sound—the unheard-of center.

For this you practiced lovely steps alone,
hoping, one day, to turn your friend's own
face and way toward that perfect celebration.

29

Stiller Freund der vielen Fernen, fühle,
wie dein Atem noch den Raum vermehrt.
Im Gebälk der finstern Glockenstühle
lass dich läuten. Das, was an dir zehrt,

wird ein Starkes über dieser Nahrung.
Geh in der Verwandlung aus und ein.
Was ist deine leidendste Erfahrung?
Ist dir Trinken bitter, werde Wein.

Sei in dieser Nacht aus Übermass
Zauberkraft am Kreuzweg deiner Sinne,
ihrer seltsamen Begegnung Sinn.

Und wenn dich das Irdische vergass,
zu der stillen Erde sag: Ich rinne.
Zu dem raschen Wasser sprich: Ich bin.

29

Silent friend of many distances, feel
how your breath is enlarging space.
Among the rafters of dark belfries
let yourself ring. What preys on you will

strengthen from such nourishment.
Come and go with metamorphosis.
What's your most painful experience?
If what you drink's bitter, turn to wine.

In this huge night, become
the magic at the crossways of your senses.
Be what their strange encounter means.

And if the earthly forgets you,
say to the quiet earth: I flow.
Speak to the rushing water—say: I am.

NOTES

115

and definitions of Part One, confidently knowledgeable about the dual world they present.

5–7. The "flower" sequence. Comparable to the fruit group of Part One, though again able to "assume" more from the reader.

8–9. Poems that seem at first glance sharply contrasted in their treatments of innocence and suffering, Rilke is taking large risks here, and it is easy to misunderstand him.

10. A "machine" sonnet that is less querulous than those in the first part. The confidence of the sestet is particularly impressive.

11. More riskiness. Rilke is not defending hunting and killing, but trying to make a place for them as facts in the existence he has defined as his poetic terrain.

12. A carefully placed summary. Homage to Ovid, possibly also to Petrarch (who punned on his Laura's name as "laurel").

13. Another summary. The wide arc that Rilke swings here takes in poet, god, and reader.

14. Flowers and gravity. Compare I, 4.

15. The ancient fountain corresponds to the sarcophagi-troughs of I, 10. The two sonnets demonstrate the imaginative mastery with which Rilke combines the material and spiritual worlds in the sequence.

16. Another startling definition.

17. Recapitulation of the fruit and flower themes.

18. Again, matter and spirit, visible and invisible, defined as a unity, with images from earlier sonnets: dancer, tree, fruit, pitcher, blossom.

19. Social misery enters the sequence through the image of the beggar.

20. Again, familiar images in a magnificent summary.

21. It helps to recall that oriental carpets are abstract depictions of ideal gardens.

22. Distinguishing among kinds of excess. Haste is mostly waste. Architectural ornaments—caryatids, bells, a column supporting nothing—are another matter.

23. Unusual intimacy between poet and reader. Or poem and reader. Recapitulation of praise theme and of the paradoxical sense of existence.

24. Spring again, and renewal.

25. One of the best spring poems ever written.

26. Even as he "prays" for the transformation of suffering to beauty, noise to music, the speaker is accomplishing it. After Orpheus was torn apart, his head and lyre, carried down the river to a sacred cave, continued to make music.

27. Death, like Time, may well be an illusion we suffer from instead of a terrible reality.

28. The dancer and the god, mortal and immortal, come together. They also come and go.

29. Addressed most of all to the reader.

ABOUT THE AUTHOR

Rainer Maria Rilke was born in Prague in 1875. After a motley education at military and business schools and at Prague's Charles University, he travelled in Europe, Russia, Egypt, and Tunisia. In addition to *Sonnets to Orpheus*, Rilke's works include the *Duino Elegies, The Book of Pictures, Poems from the Book of Hours, New Poems,* and *The Notebook of Malte Laurids Brigge*. Rilke died in 1926.

ABOUT THE TRANSLATOR

David Young is a poet and scholar, as well as a translator. He is Longman Professor of English at Oberlin College; co-editor of the literary magazine *Field;* arbiter of *Field's* translation series; translator of Chinese, German, Italian, and Czechoslovakian poetry; and a Shakespearean scholar. His book *The Planet on the Desk: New and Selected Poems, 1960–1990* was published by Wesleyan in 1991.